HOT WHEELS DEVELOPER

Elliot Handler

JESSIE ALKIRE

Checkerboard
Library

An Imprint of Abdo Publishing
abdobooks.com

abdobooks.com

Published by Abdo Publishing, a division of ABDO, PO Box 398166, Minneapolis, Minnesota 55439. Copyright © 2019 by Abdo Consulting Group, Inc. International copyrights reserved in all countries. No part of this book may be reproduced in any form without written permission from the publisher. Checkerboard Library™ is a trademark and logo of Abdo Publishing.

Printed in the United States of America, North Mankato, Minnesota
102018
012019

Design and Production: Mighty Media, Inc.
Editor: Rebecca Felix
Cover Photographs: Getty Images (center); Mighty Media, Inc.
Interior Photographs: Antoine Carolus/UkeHeidi, p. 11; AP Images, pp. 9, 28 (bottom); Courtesy of Mattel, pp. 17, 20; Courtesy of The Strong, Rochester, New York, pp. 21, 29 (top); Curtis Palmer/Flickr, pp. 18, 28 (top); Getty Images, pp. 13, 22, 27; iStockphoto, pp. 7, 12, 23, 25, 29 (middle); John Morgan/Flickr, p. 19; Robert Couse-Baker/Flickr, p. 14; Shutterstock, pp. 5, 16, 26, 29 (bottom); Tons-of-Toys.com, p. 24; Voss Vintage Chic, Connie Voss, p. 10; Wikimedia Commons, p. 15

Library of Congress Control Number: 2018948788

Publisher's Cataloging-in-Publication Data
Names: Alkire, Jessie, author.
Title: Hot Wheels developer: Elliot Handler / by Jessie Alkire.
Other title: Elliot Handler
Description: Minneapolis, Minnesota : Abdo Publishing, 2019 | Series: Toy
    trailblazers set 3 | Includes online resources and index.
Identifiers: ISBN 9781532117084 (lib. bdg.) | ISBN 9781532159923 (ebook)
Subjects: LCSH: Handler, Elliot--Juvenile literature. | Inventors--United States--
    Biography--Juvenile literature. | Hot Wheels toys--Juvenile literature. |
    Toymakers--Biography--Juvenile literature.
Classification: DDC 688.72092 [B]--dc23

CONTENTS

CAR CREATOR

Chapter 1

Hot Wheels cars are some of the most popular and famous toys in history. More than 4 billion of them have been produced! The cars are made by well-known toy company Mattel. Elliot Handler is the cofounder of Mattel and the inventor of Hot Wheels.

Isadore Elliot Handler was born on April 9, 1916, in Chicago, Illinois. His parents, Samuel and Freida, were **immigrants**. They were both born in what is now Ukraine.

Samuel immigrated to the United States in 1906. Freida came to the country in 1914. That year, Samuel and Freida were married. They moved to Chicago to start a family. Soon, the couple had three children, Albert, Isadore, and Sylvia.

Isadore would eventually go by his middle name, Elliot. But when he was young, he went by the **nickname** "Izzy." When Izzy was three years old, Samuel caught **tuberculosis**. Samuel needed to live somewhere with cleaner air to ease his **symptoms**. So, the family moved to Denver, Colorado. They lived there for the rest of Izzy's childhood.

Elliot Handler's dream of making toy cars with speed, power, performance, and cool design came to life with Hot Wheels.

Chapter 2

ARTIST
in the Making

Izzy was a creative child. **He was interested in art and wanted to** become a cartoonist. By his teenage years, Izzy was making money doing creative work. He had a part-time job helping make light fixtures.

In 1932, Izzy met Ruth Mosko at a dance. The two danced together all night and soon began dating. After high school, Izzy attended art school in Denver. Ruth also attended college in Denver before deciding to move to California.

It wasn't long before Izzy joined Ruth in California. He attended the Art Center School in Los Angeles. He also worked for another company designing light fixtures.

Ruth and Handler married in 1938. They moved into an apartment in the Hollywood neighborhood of Los Angeles. The apartment included a garage shared by several tenants. Hander used the garage as a as a workshop. He began experimenting with a kind of plastic called Lucite.

Lucite is a brand name for an acrylic resin first created in the 1930s. In the following decades, Lucite became a popular material for furniture, jewelry, and more.

Chapter 3

FAMILY
Business

Handler's workshop soon filled with decorative products he'd created out of Lucite. He made lamps, picture frames, mirrors, and more. Handler and Ruth decided to start a business selling the products. But soon after, their neighbor complained about how the Handlers were using the shared garage. The apartment manager told the Handlers they couldn't use the garage for their workshop.

So, the Handlers decided to move production to a new facility. Handler left school and quit his job to make his products full time. Ruth sold the products. They called the company Elliot Handler Plastics.

In May 1939, the Handlers made their first sale! Their business continued to attract new customers over the next two years. Then, the Handlers met a jeweler named Zachary Zemby. Together, Zemby and the Handlers formed a new costume jewelry company called Elzac.

Handler's talent for developing products matched well with Ruth's talents for marketing. The couple were successful business partners.

As the Handlers' business grew, so did their family. Their first child, Barbara, was born in May 1941. Their second child, Ken, came three years later. Ruth left the business to raise their children.

Chapter 4

TURNING to Toys

By 1944, Elzac was earning $2 million each year. However, the company's investors often disagreed about how the company should operate. One of Elzac's employees, Harold "Matt" Matson, was tired of the arguments. So, he quit. Soon after, Handler decided to follow Matson.

In 1945, the Handlers and Matson started a new company called Mattel Creations. The company name was later shortened to Mattel. At first, Mattel sold wooden picture frames.

Elzac jewelry sold for up to $9 an item in the 1940s. Today, these items are collectibles. Collectors often pay more than $100 for one Elzac find!

Uke-A-Doodle

As the frames became popular, Handler used the leftover scraps from the frames to make doll furniture.

Handler's doll furniture was even more successful than the frames. Because of this, Mattel shifted its focus to toys. The company's first successful toy was the Uke-A-Doodle, a child-sized **ukulele**. The musical toy was released in 1947.

After the Uke-A-Doodle's release, Matson sold his portion of the business to the Handlers. Handler continued to design new toys while Ruth **marketed** and sold the products. Mattel soon released music boxes, jack-in-the-boxes, and dolls.

FUN FACT

In 1955, the Handlers began advertising their toys on the popular children's television show *The Mickey Mouse Club*. A year's worth of ads cost $500,000. But the price was worth it. Mattel's profits skyrocketed!

Chapter 5

Barbie SUCCESS

Handler was the brains behind most of Mattel's products. But in 1959, it was Ruth who had a grand idea. Ruth noticed that their daughter, Barbara, loved paper dolls. Barbara made her dolls act like adults rather than children. Ruth decided Mattel should create a **3-D** teenage doll. She named the doll Barbie, which was her daughter's **nickname**.

Barbie was immediately popular. Within a year, more than 350,000 Barbie dolls were sold. Mattel also released separate sets of Barbie outfits. Ruth wanted girls to be able to act out their dreams for the future with Barbie dolls.

In 1961, Mattel introduced a male 3-D teenage doll named Ken. Ken was Barbie's companion. He was named after the Handlers' son.

Ruth and Handler hold the original Barbie and Ken dolls.

Over the next several years, Mattel released other Barbie friends and outfit sets. The company also created educational toys, such as See 'N Say. This toy helped children learn language and sounds.

By 1965, Mattel's sales reached more than $100 million. The company also joined the Fortune 500, a list of the world's largest companies.

Ken

Chapter 6

A HOT IDEA

The 1960s were full of successes for the Handlers and Mattel. Handler was determined to create a toy that was as popular with boys as Barbie was with girls. In 1966, he noticed his grandchild playing with **die-cast** toy cars. After this, Handler started thinking about **miniature** cars.

Small die-cast cars were popular toys in the 1950s and 1960s. But they didn't move as well or look as exciting as Handler thought they could. He wanted to create stylish miniature **vehicles** that could move quickly when pushed.

To make his dream a reality, Handler hired Harry Bradley. Bradley was an automobile designer at General Motors. Bradley and his team designed a series of miniature cars. Handler reviewed every design. He wanted the cars to look **exotic** and imaginative.

Die-cast cars made by Dinky Toys in the 1950s. Before Hot Wheels,
Dinky Toys were among the most popular die-cast toy cars in history.

Handler named his cars Hot Wheels. He wanted Hot Wheels cars to move like real automobiles. So, Handler and his team developed a wheel system that made this possible.

The wheels were made of plastic and had rubberlike outer layers. The tiny **wheel bearings** were made of Delrin, a strong, low-**friction** plastic. The **axles** were as thin as possible and connected to the center of the car.

The wheel system gave Hot Wheels their speed. The system was also **unique** among other toy cars being sold at the time. Mattel had officially set its cars apart from competitors' products!

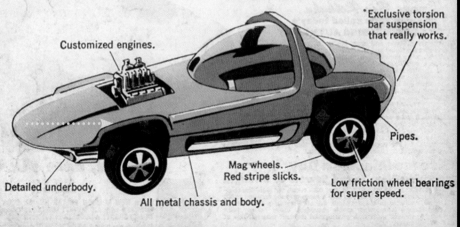

New from Mattel. The fastest miniature cars you've ever seen. And look at these features!

Customized engines.

* Exclusive torsion bar suspension that really works.

Pipes.

Mag wheels.
Red stripe slicks.

Low friction wheel bearings for super speed.

Detailed underbody.

All metal chassis and body.

Choose from 16 new California custom styled Hot Wheels!

Advertisements for the first 16 Hot Wheels models described the vehicles' unique features.

Chapter 7

MADE for Play

Hot Wheels had style and speed unlike any other **miniature** cars. Now, Handler had to see if the cars would sell! Hot Wheels production began in 1967.

Production took a long time. Each car had many parts that had to be made and assembled by hand. But Mattel's factories were soon making more than 200,000 cars each week!

After the cars were assembled, each was painted with bright, eye-catching colors. After the paint dried, workers picked cars at **random** for testing. These chosen cars were sent down a track. Workers made sure the cars traveled at least 50 feet (15 m) without stopping.

A Custom Camaro with dark blue paint was one of the first Hot Wheels cars produced.

Handler's team also developed a bright orange track on which players could race Hot Wheels.

After testing, Hot Wheels cars were packaged in clear plastic. This way, customers could see exactly what they were buying. Hot Wheels was one of the first brands among its competitors to use this type of packaging.

Chapter 8

Selling HOT

Hot Wheels were released in 1968. The first line had 16 different models of cars. The fast-moving, attractive Hot Wheels cars were a huge hit. Mattel earned $25 million from Hot Wheels sales in 1968. Sixteen million Hot Wheels were sold that year!

In 1969, Mattel released 24 more Hot Wheels models. Its designers and engineers were also hard at work creating a new line of Hot Wheels.

The new line was called Sizzlers and released in 1970. These cars had small motors and batteries. Unlike regular Hot Wheels, Sizzlers could move without being pushed. They could even drive uphill! Kids could recharge the cars with a power station called the Power Pit.

FUN FACT

The most valued Hot Wheels vehicle is a 1969 Volkswagen Beach Bomb. It is a pink van with surfboards sticking out of the back. One van sold for $125,000!

Sizzlers ran on the original orange Hot Wheels track, but Mattel also created special tracks with spirals and loops that the Sizzlers could power through.

This is the fastest car in the world. It's only 3 inches long. It's a Hot Wheels® Sizzlers® with a real engine.

It goes at a scale speed that's faster than the speed of sound. This "supersonic" speed is guaranteed by a *lifetime* electric power cell right inside the car. You recharge it with the JUICE MACHINE™ or POWER PIT.®

This is the wildest, fastest car ever made. And there are 8 different models complete with exciting racing layouts and plenty of accessories.

HOT WHEELS® SIZZLERS.® No other model car can touch them.

Chapter 9

HOT WHEELS
Hits

Throughout the 1970s, Mattel continued to release new models of the original Hot Wheels cars. The company also produced new Sizzlers, construction **vehicles**, and trucks under the Hot Wheels

American collector Bruce Pascal owns more than 3,500 Hot Wheels cars! His collection is valued at more than $1 million.

Hot Wheels has released several Batmobiles, the car superhero Batman drives.

TV SERIES BATMOBILE™

brand. However, by 1975, the Handlers were having conflicts with other leaders at Mattel. That year, Handler and Ruth resigned from the company.

Hot Wheels continued to succeed without the Handlers. In 1979, Mattel partnered with Marvel Comics to create superhero **vehicles**. These vehicles had comic book characters painted on the sides. Some of these vehicles were called Scene Machines. Scene Machines had a small window kids could look into to see an image of the superhero inside the vehicle.

In the 1980s, Hot Wheels remained a popular toy for children. But now, adults also bought the cars for themselves as collectibles! Mattel released a collector's handbook to appeal to these customers. Collectors could use the handbook to see all Hot Wheels models. Hot Wheels collector **conventions** were held in the 1980s as well. These conventions allowed collectors to meet and discuss all things Hot Wheels.

In 1983, Mattel released 20 new Hot Wheels models. It also created a new Hot Wheels line called Extras. Buyers could **customize** these cars with additional parts. In 1988, Mattel released Color Racers. These cars' paint changed colors in hot or cold water!

Temperature changes turned Color Racers' paint different colors in seconds!

FOR AGES OVER 5.
DIE-CAST METAL BODIES!

MICRO COLOR RACERS

PAINT-CHANGING SPEED MACHINES!

Cars change colors instantly! All it takes is icy cold & warm water!

RACE PACK

ULTRA FAST!

3226

WARNING: CONTAINS SMALL PARTS

Mattel has made more than 100 Star Wars Hot Wheels toys over the years!

In 1991, Hot Wheels produced its one-billionth car. The brand celebrated by releasing a collection of four toy Corvettes made with gold chrome. Ten years later, Hot Wheels created a drivable, life-sized Hot Wheels car. The **replica** was displayed at an auto show in Las Vegas, Nevada. Hot Wheels has since produced 20 other life-sized drivable replicas.

The 2000s saw many more partnerships between Hot Wheels and other companies. In 2002, Mattel partnered with DC Comics to produce Hot Wheels based on popular comic book characters or their **vehicles**.

In 2010, Hot Wheels partnered with Disney-Pixar's *Toy Story 3* movie to create Character Cars. These cars were styled with the recognizable features of characters from the movie. The Character Cars line expanded through partnerships with Marvel Studios, Star Wars, and other well-known brands.

FUN FACT

Hot Wheels were often offered as McDonald's Happy Meal toys in the 1990s.

Chapter 10

LEAVING
a Legacy

Mattel's partnerships helped maintain the popularity of Hot Wheels. Though Handler was no longer part of Mattel, he still took pride in Hot Wheels' success. The Handlers were **inducted** into the Toy Industry Hall of Fame in 1989. They were the first living people to receive the honor.

Handler died on July 21, 2011, at age 95. Hot Wheels were inducted into the National Toy Hall of Fame the same year. Mattel employees remember Handler as kind. He made them feel valued and respected.

Founding Mattel was Handler's greatest success. Today, it is one of the world's largest toy companies. And Hot Wheels is one of the company's most successful brands. In 2018, Mattel celebrated 50 years

Chevy's 2018 Hot Wheels Camaro replica

Handler and his daughter at a 2003 Hot Wheels event. Handler's brother said his sibling was a ". . . quiet, kind man. I think that's why he liked toys so much. They make people happy."

of Hot Wheels. US car manufacturer Chevrolet released a full-size **replica** of the Hot Wheels Camaro for the occasion!

Hot Wheels continue to be a popular toy and collectible item. They are even used in the classroom! Speedometry is a program that uses Hot Wheels to teach science and math to young students. Whether at home or in the classroom, Handler's **legacy** lives on in Hot Wheels cars.

TIMELINE

1916

Isadore Elliot Handler is born in Chicago, Illinois.

1945

The Handlers and Harold Matson create Mattel. The company sells picture frames but soon change its focus to toys.

1967

Hot Wheels are first produced. The first 16 car models are released the following year.

1938

Handler marries Ruth Mosko. The two soon begin a business making plastic products.

1959

Mattel's most successful product, the Barbie doll, is released.

1970

Hot Wheels Sizzlers are released. They are the first Hot Wheels cars to have motors.

1975

The Handlers resign from Mattel.

2000

Hot Wheels partners with brands such as Marvel Studios and Star Wars to create themed cars.

2011

Handler dies at age 95. Hot Wheels are inducted into the National Toy Hall of Fame.

1991

Mattel produces its one-billionth Hot Wheels car.

2018

Hot Wheels celebrates its fiftieth anniversary. Chevrolet releases a full-size replica of the Hot Wheels Camaro.

Glossary

axle – a shaft or a bar on which wheels revolve.

convention – a group of people meeting for a special purpose.

customize – to make or change something to fit individual preferences.

die-cast – made by a process of forcing liquid metal into a mold.

exotic – interesting because it is strange or different from the usual.

friction – the force that resists motion between bodies in contact.

immigrant – a person who enters another country to live. To enter another country to live is to immigrate.

induct – to admit as a member.

legacy – something important or meaningful handed down from previous generations or from the past.

market – to advertise or promote it so people will want to buy it. This process is called marketing.

miniature – a copy of something in a reduced size.

nickname – a name given to someone that is different than that person's original name.

random – lacking a definite plan or pattern.

replica – an exact copy.

Booklinks
NONFICTION
NETWORK
FREE! ONLINE NONFICTION RESOURCES

ONLINE RESOURCES

To learn more about Elliot Handler and Hot Wheels, visit **abdobooklinks.com.** These links are routinely monitored and updated to provide the most current information available.

symptom – a noticeable change in the normal working of the body. A symptom indicates or accompanies disease, sickness, or other malfunction.

3-D – having length, width, and height. "3-D" stands for *three-dimensional*.

tuberculosis – a disease that affects the lungs.

ukulele – a small guitar originally made popular in Hawaii.

unique (yoo-NEEK) – being the only one of its kind.

vehicle – something used to carry or transport. Cars, trucks, airplanes, and boats are vehicles.

wheel bearing – a set of steel balls arranged within a metal ring in the center of a vehicle's wheel. Wheel bearings help wheels spin smoothly.

Index